LETTER TRACING FOR KIDS

NATALIE

TRACE MY NAME WORKBOOK

Lunar Glow Readers
PUBLISHING

ABOUT ME

MY NAME IS:

Natalie

I AM [ ] YEARS OLD.

I LIVE IN:

For parents

For kids

DRAW YOU AND YOUR FAMILY

N

Natalie

Natalie

Natalie

Natalie

Natalie

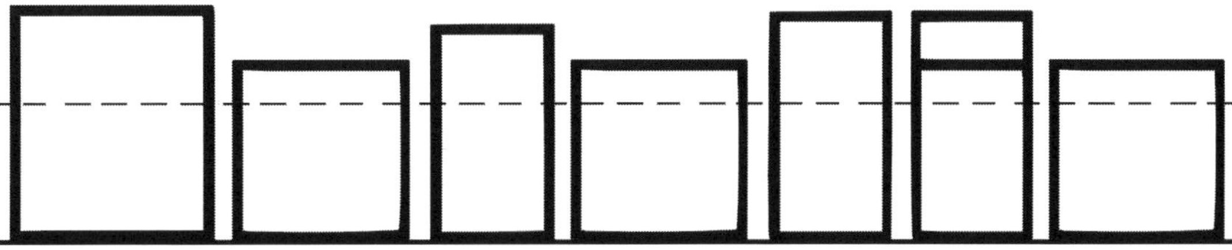

THIS IS HOW I WRITE MY NAME

MY NAME HAS ___ LETTERS

1	2	3	4	5	6	7	8

Natalie

atalie

talie

alie

lie

ie

COLOR THE EGGS WITH LETTERS OF OUR NAME WRITE YOUR NAME

P B M F I

V T D E S

Z N L C J

R A Y Q W

G U K O H

A

WRITE YOUR NAME

Natalie

WRITE YOU NAME WITH.

PEN 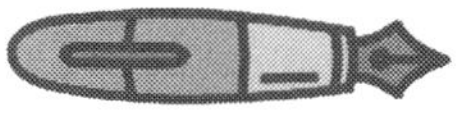

Natalie

CRAYON 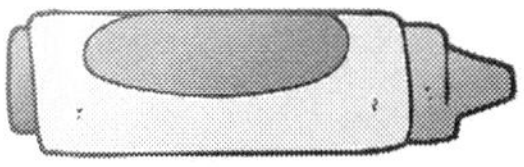

Natalie

WRITE YOUR NAME IN BLUE

Natalie

WRITE YOUR NAME IN YELLOW

Natalie

DRAW YOUR FAVORITE THINGS

COLOR

FOOD

TOY

ANIMAL

MY NAME

MY NAME STARTS WITH

____

MY NAME ENDS WITH

____

FILL THE LETTERS OF YOUR NAME WHITH DIFFERENT COLORS

P B W F V I T

D E S Z N L C

J R A Y Q K

G U A O H M

Natalie

Natalie

Natalie

Natalie

Natalie

Natalie

Natalie

Natalie

Natalie

Natalie

Natalie

Natalie

Natalie

Natalie

Natalie

Natalie

Natalie

Natalie

Natalie

Natalie

Natalie

Natalie

Natalie

Natalie

Natalie

Natalie

Natalie

Natalie

Natalie

Natalie

Natalie

Natalie

Natalie

Natalie

Natalie

Natalie

Natalie

Natalie

Natalie

Natalie

Natalie

Natalie

Natalie

Natalie

Natalie

Natalie

Natalie

Natalie

Natalie

Natalie

Natalie

Natalie

Natalie

Natalie

Natalie

Natalie

Natalie

Natalie

Natalie

Natalie

Natalie

Natalie

Natalie

Natalie

Natalie

Natalie

Natalie

Natalie

Natalie

Natalie

Natalie

Natalie

Natalie

Natalie

Natalie

N N N N

N N N N

N N N N

N N N N

N N N N

a a a a

a a a a

a a a a

a a a a

a a a a

t t t t t

t t t t t

t t t t t

t t t t t

t t t t t

a a a a

a a a a

a a a a

a a a a

a a a a

i i i i i i

i i i i i i

i i i i i i

i i i i i i

i i i i i i

e e e e

e e e e

e e e e

e e e e

e e e e

N N N N

N N N N

N N N N

N N N N

N N N N

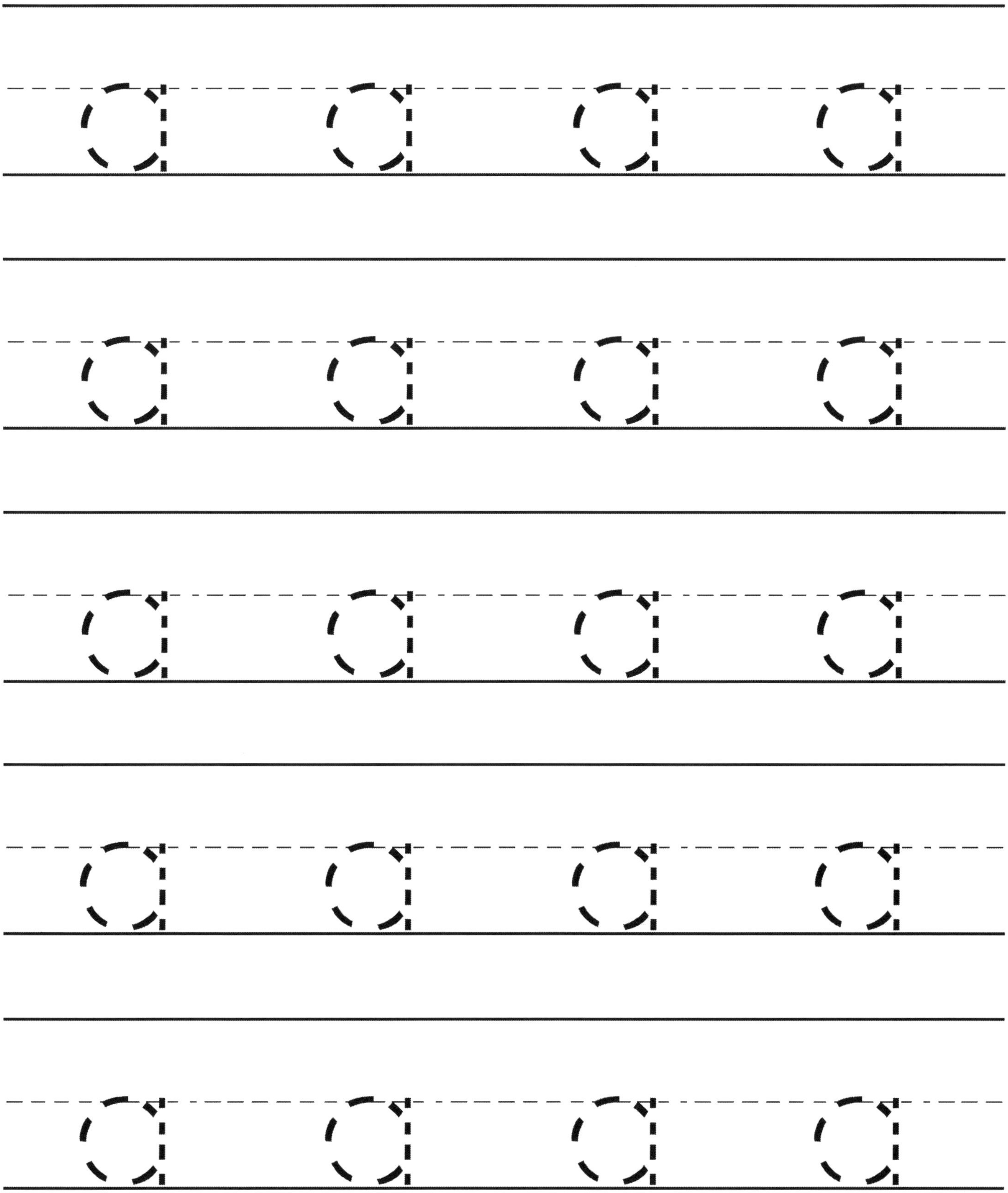
a a a a
a a a a
a a a a
a a a a
a a a a

t t t t t

t t t t t

t t t t t

t t t t t

t t t t t

a a a a

a a a a

a a a a

a a a a

a a a a

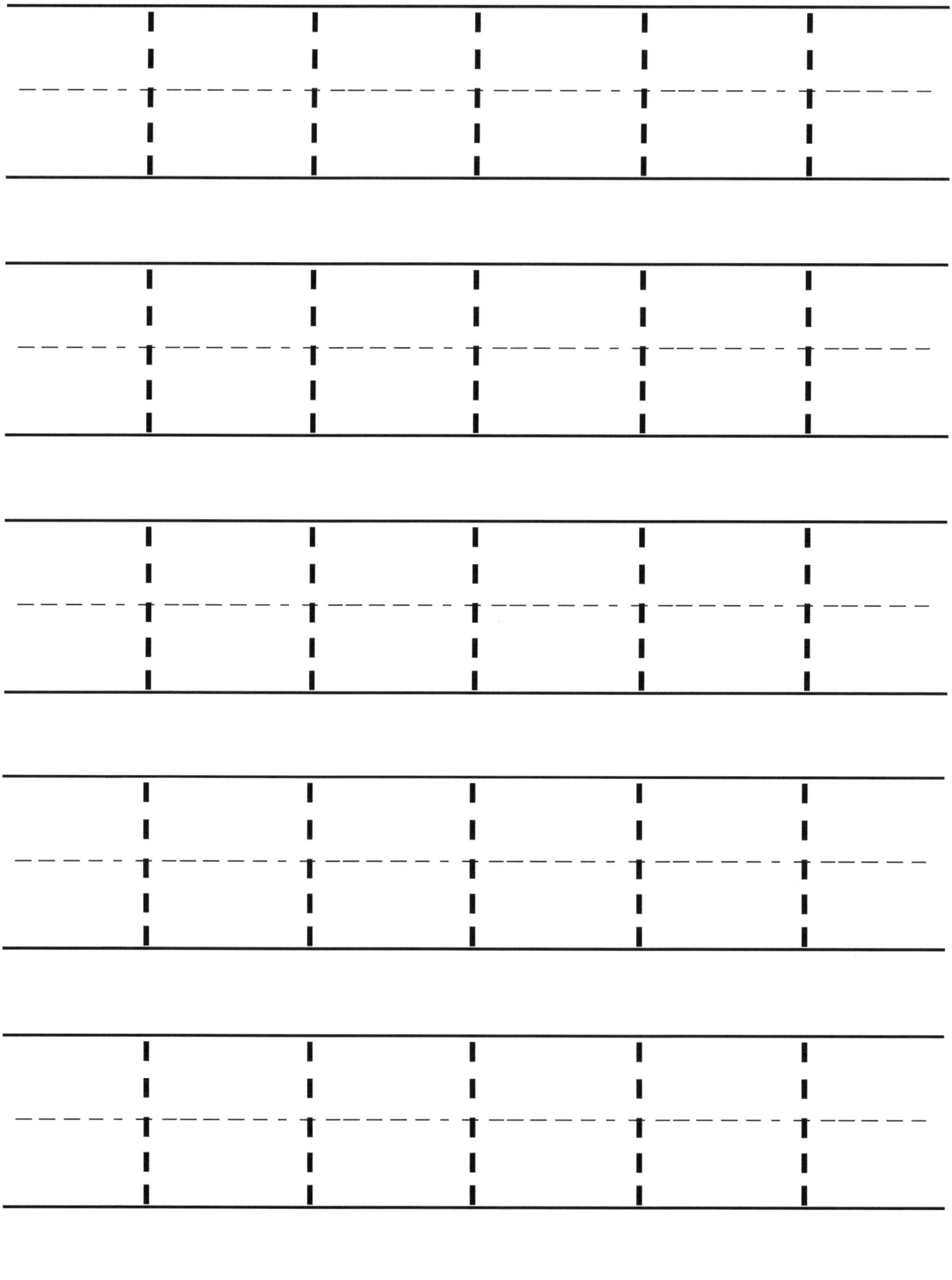

i i i i i i

i i i i i i

i i i i i i

i i i i i i

i i i i i i

e e e e

e e e e

e e e e

e e e e

e e e e

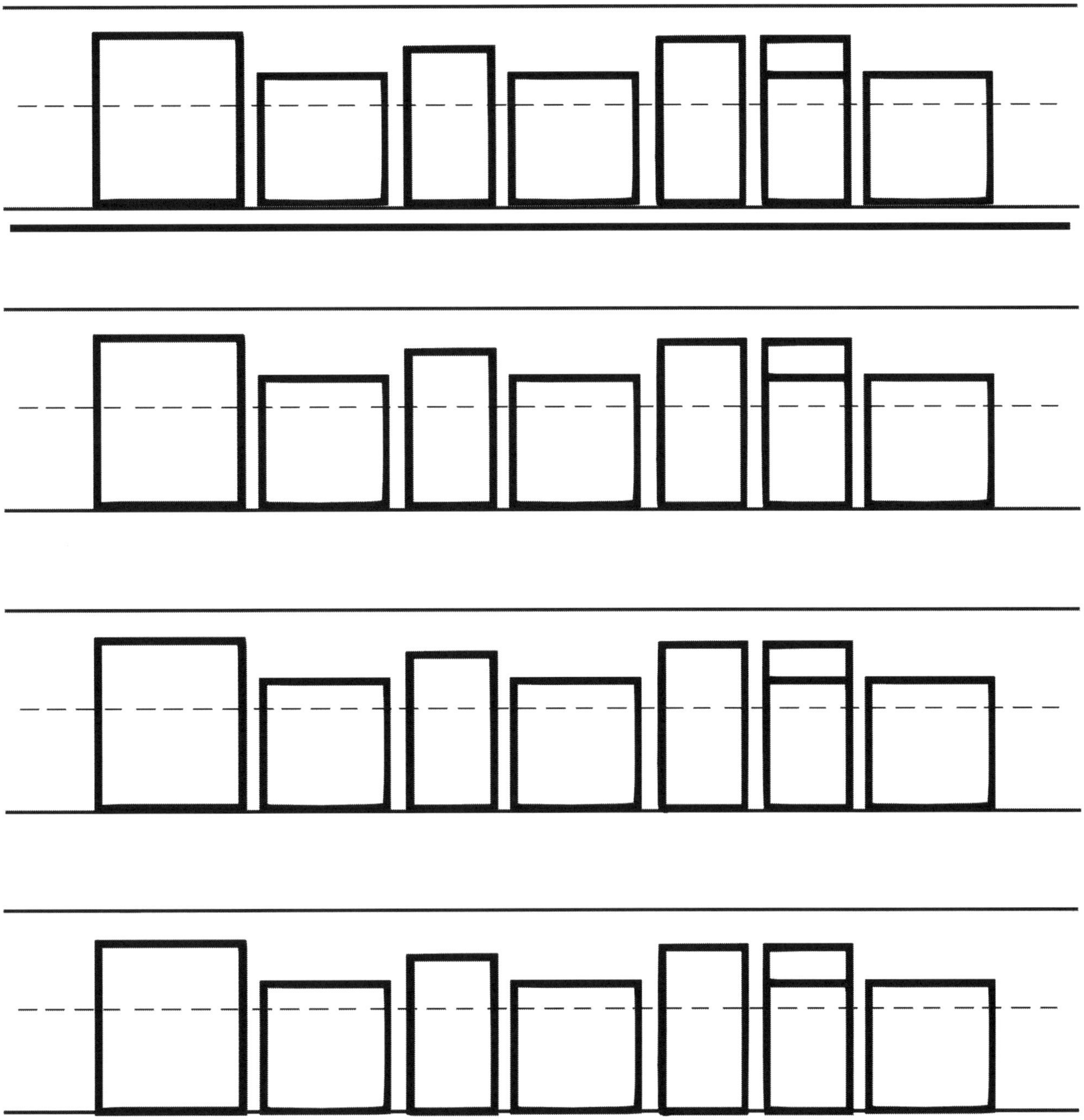

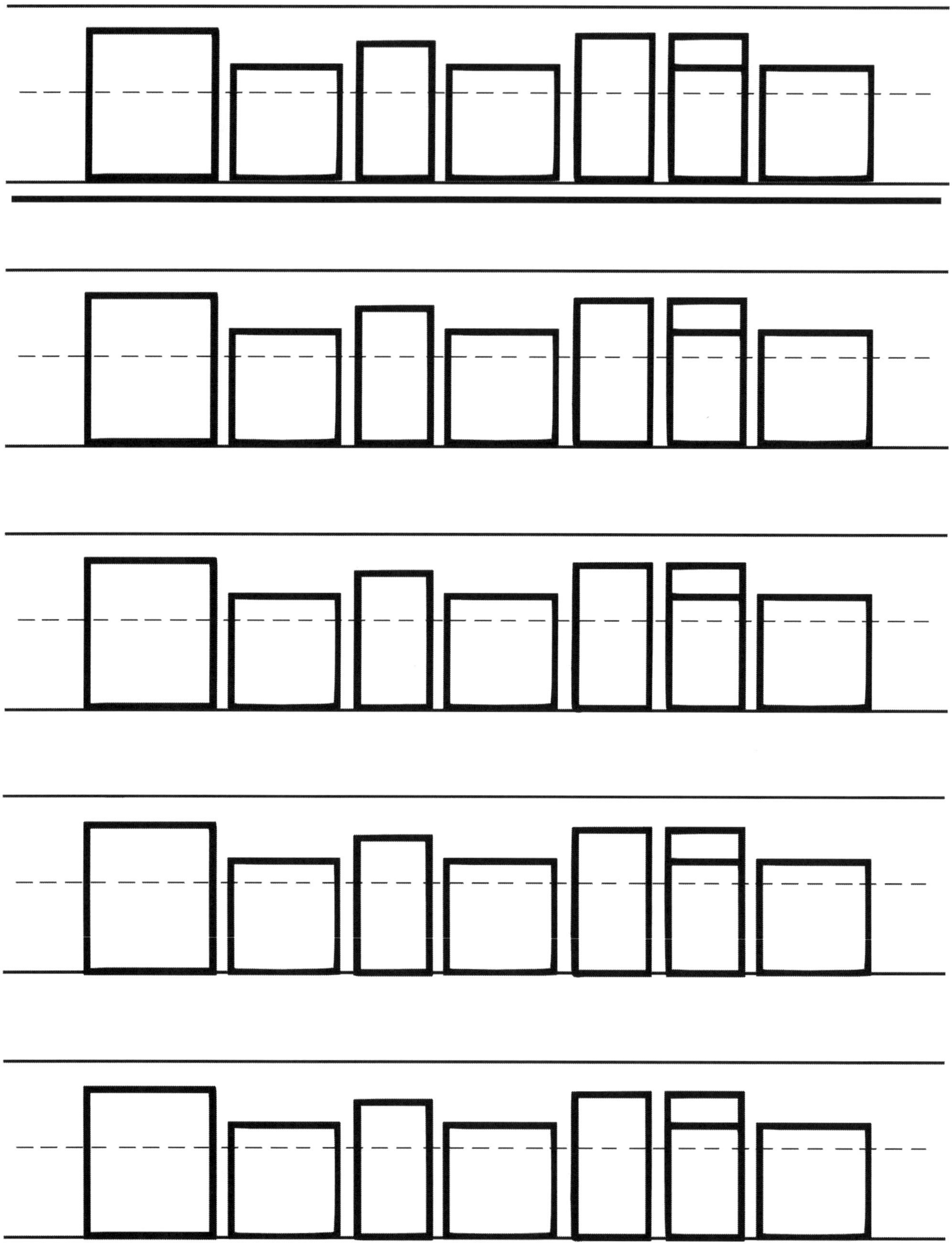

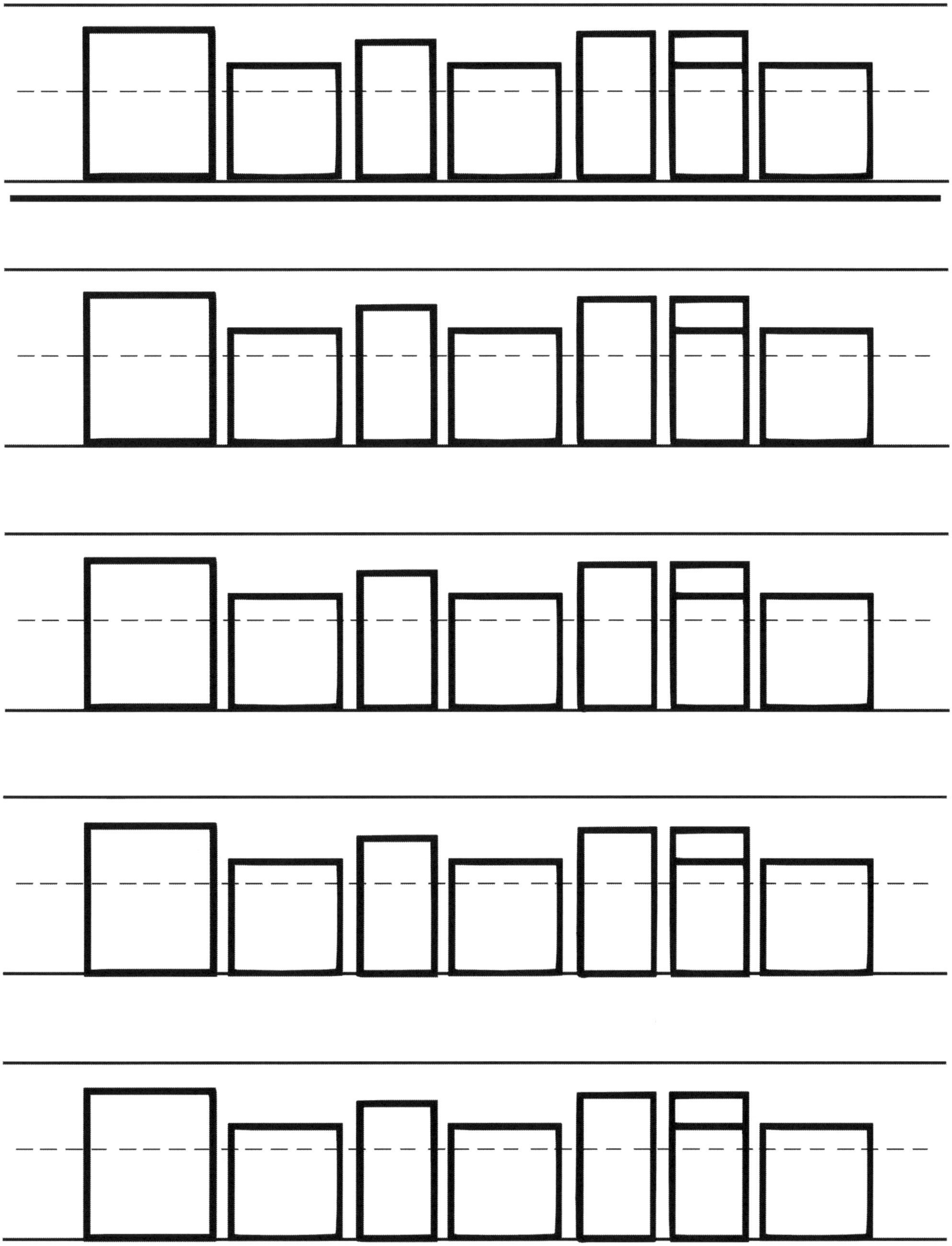

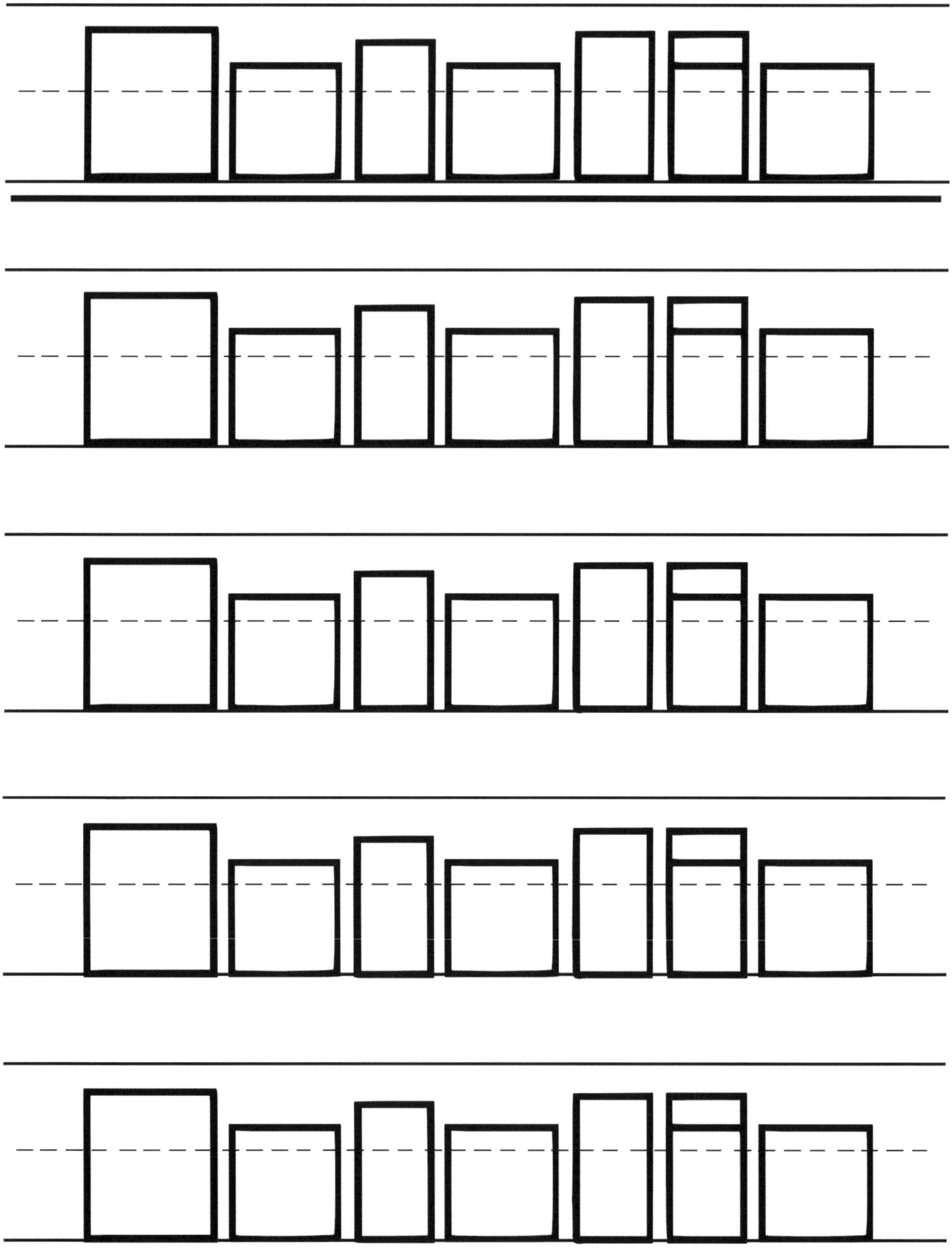

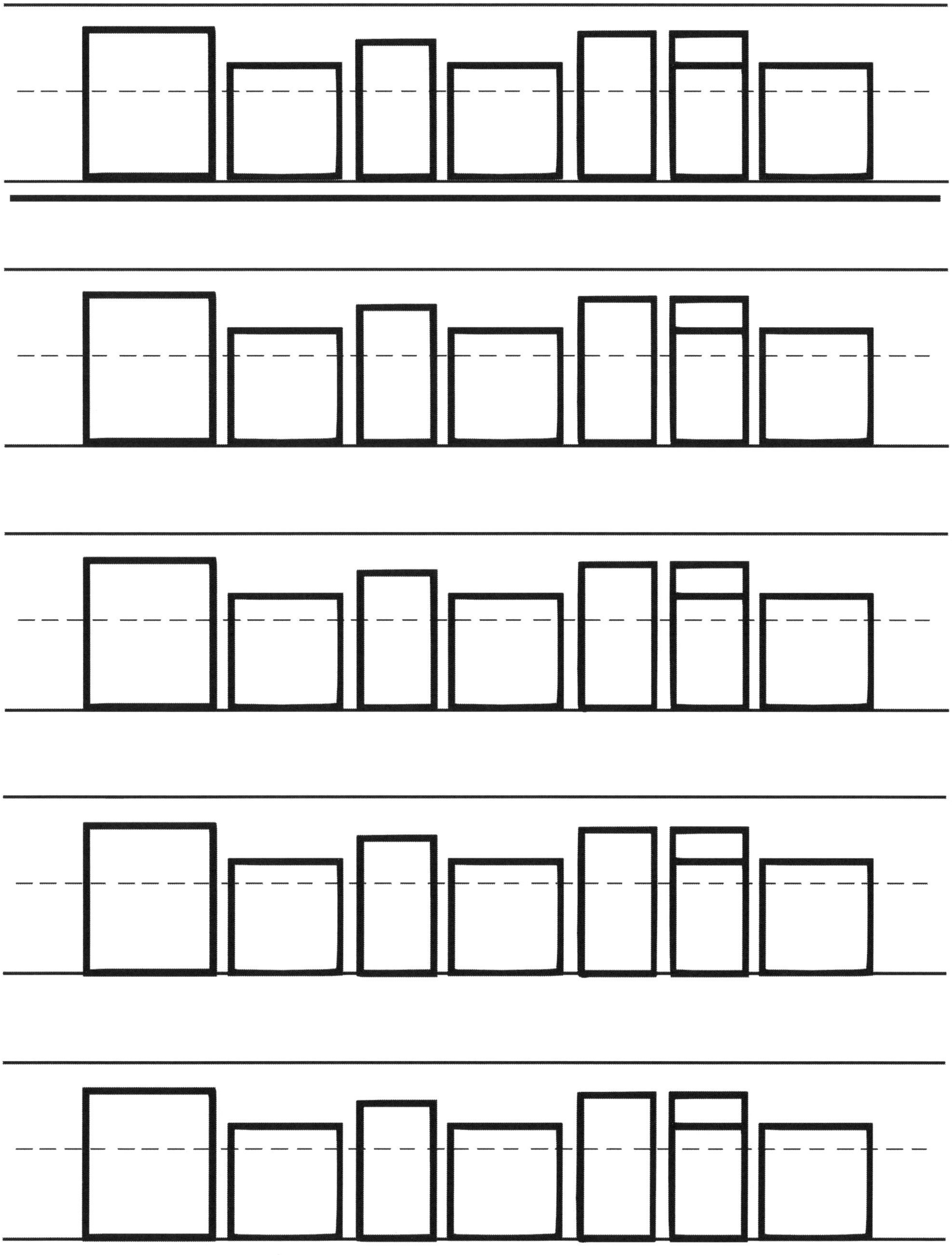

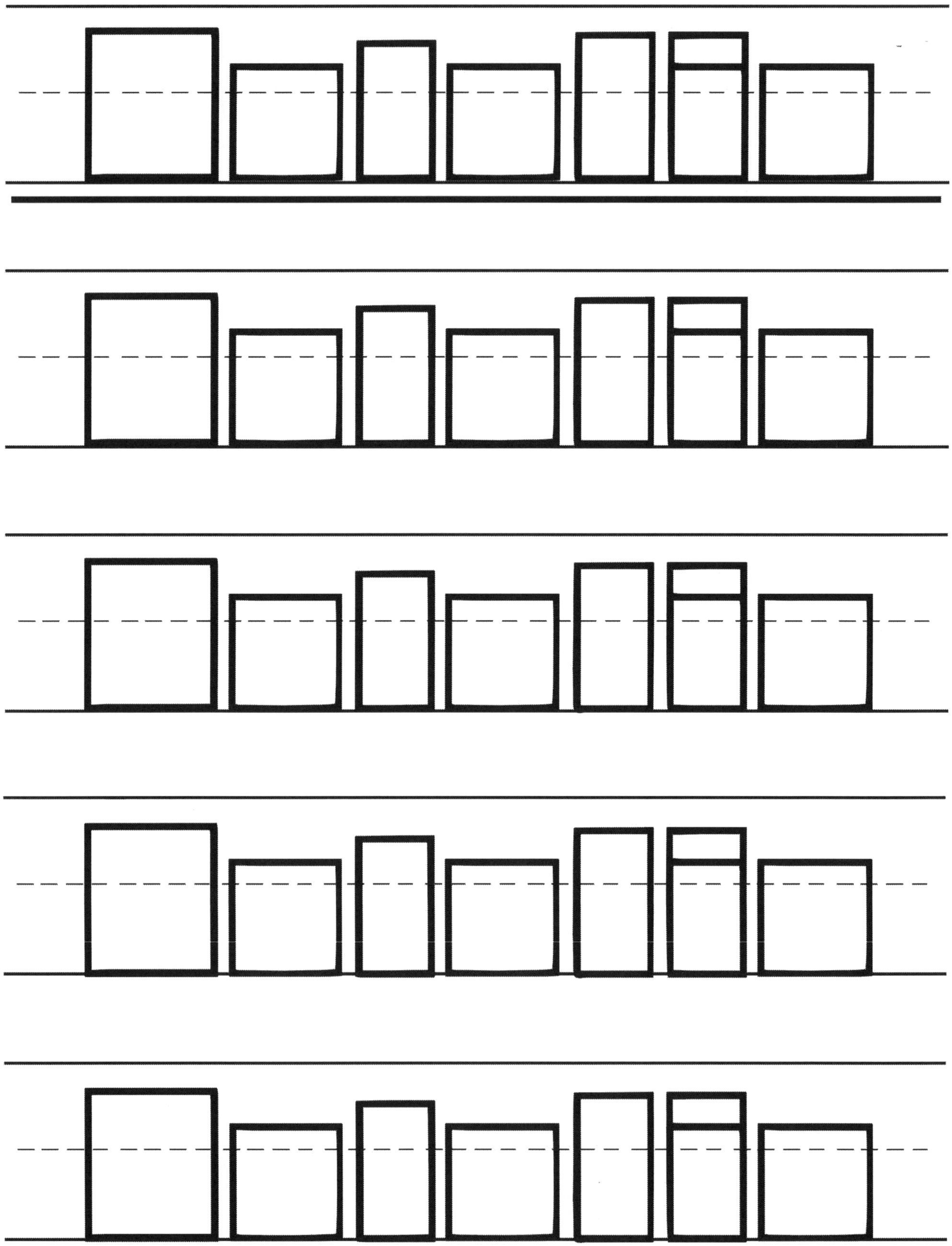

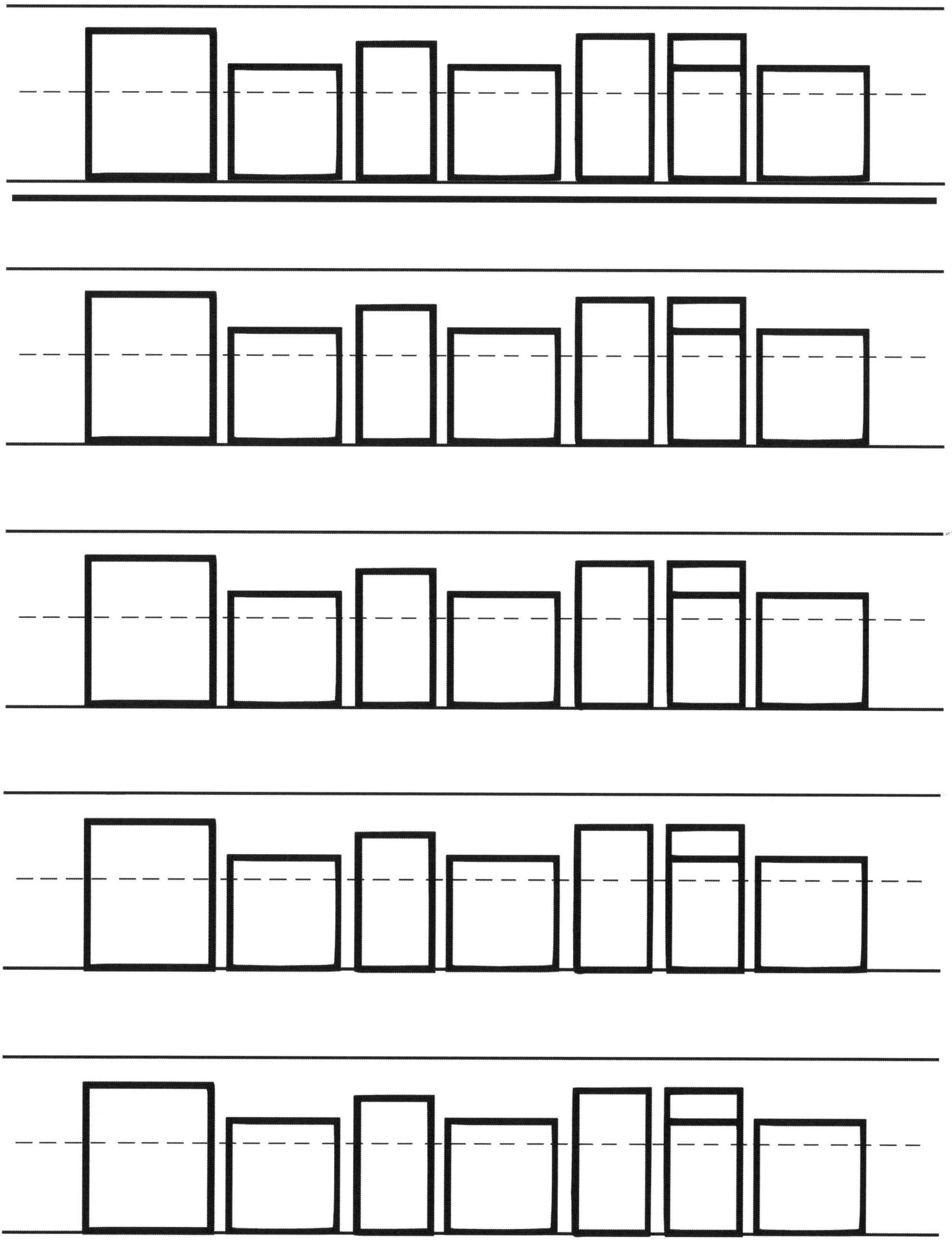

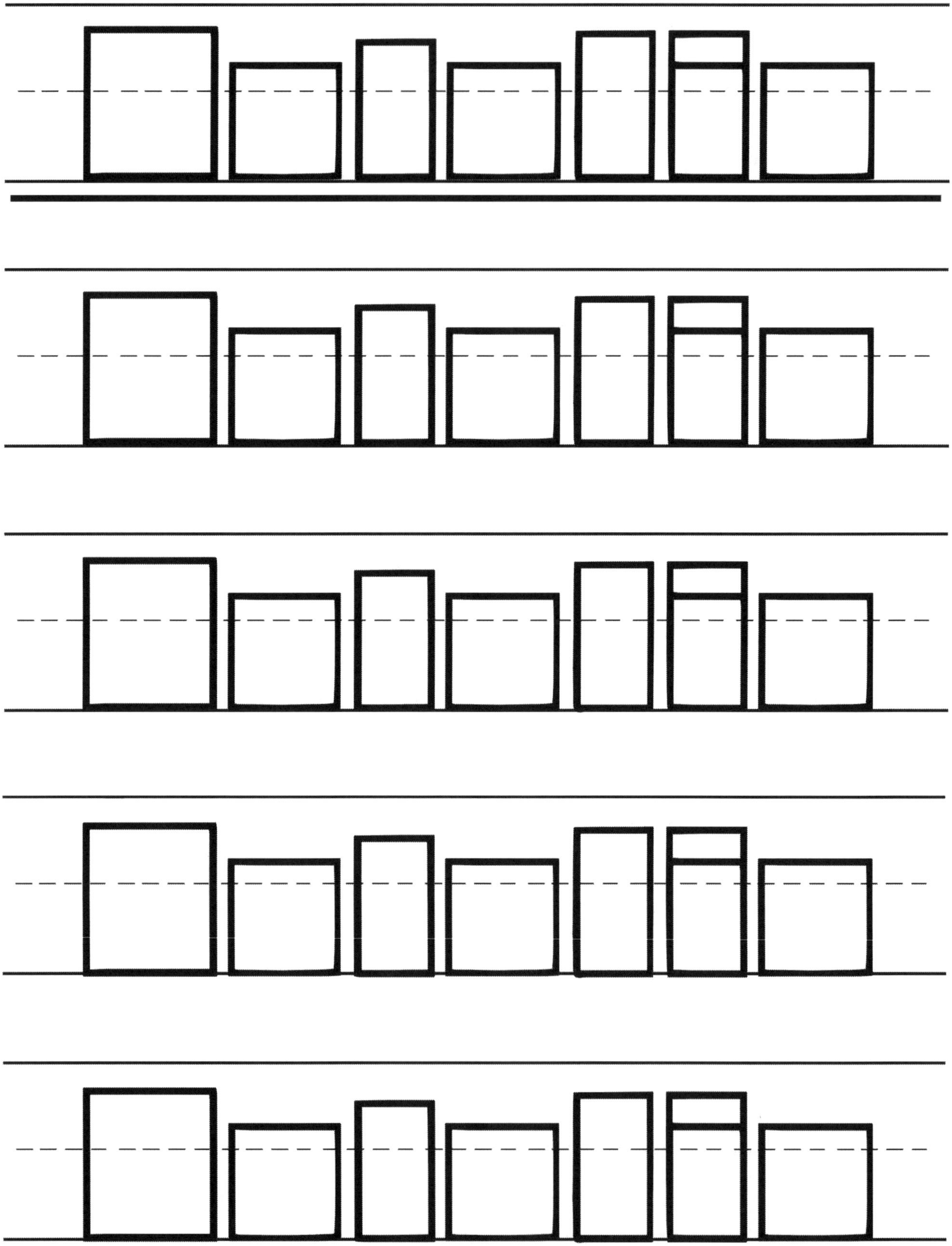

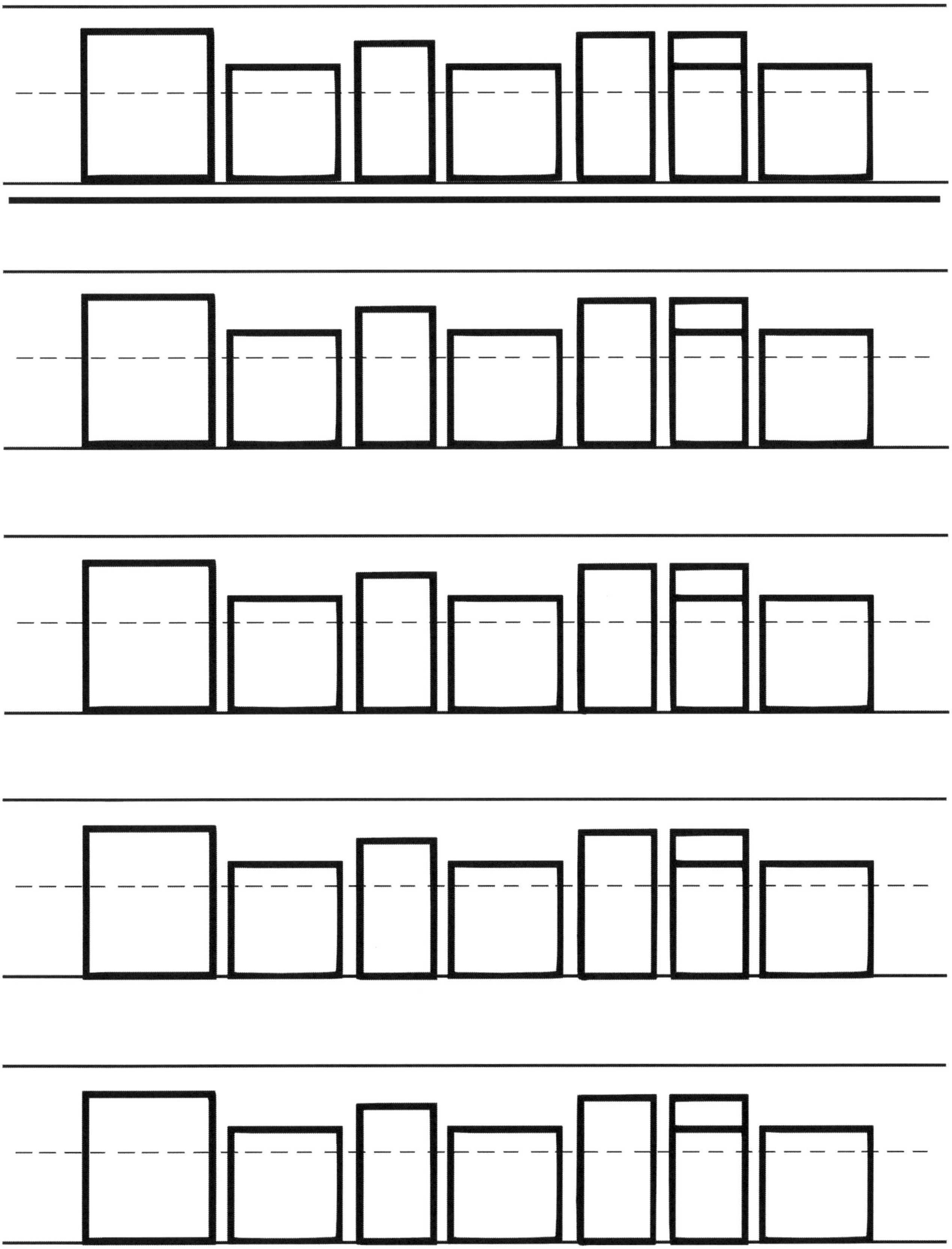

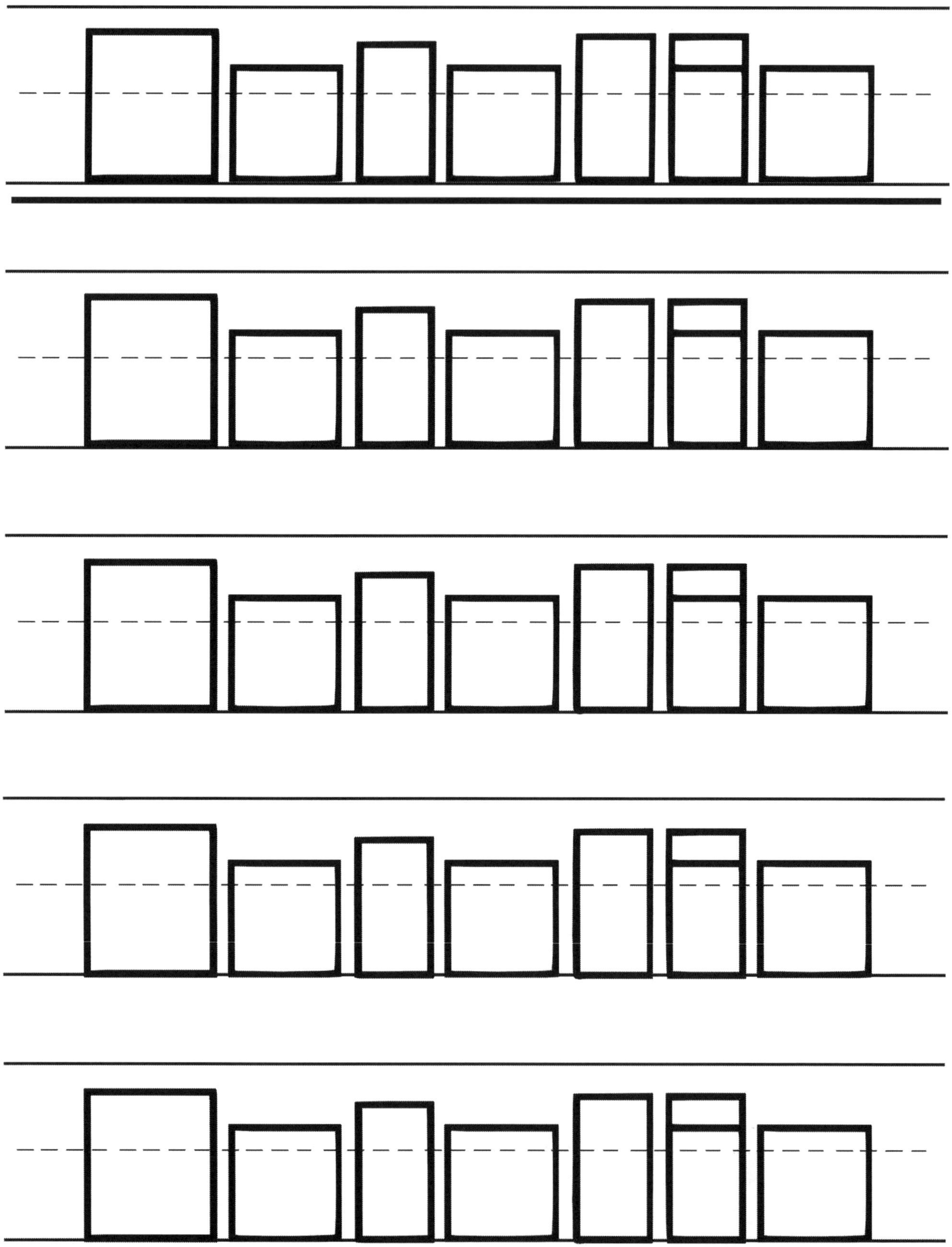

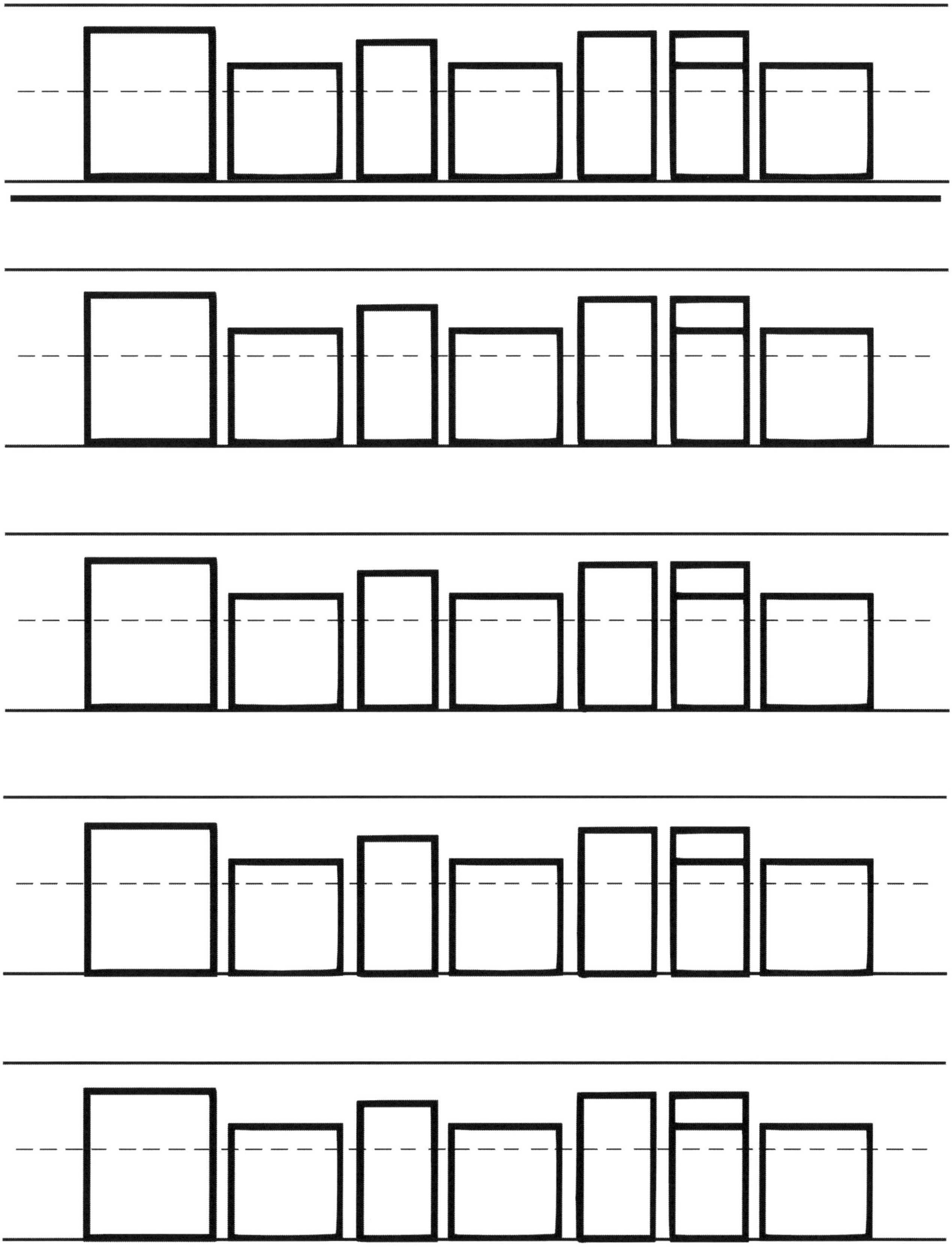

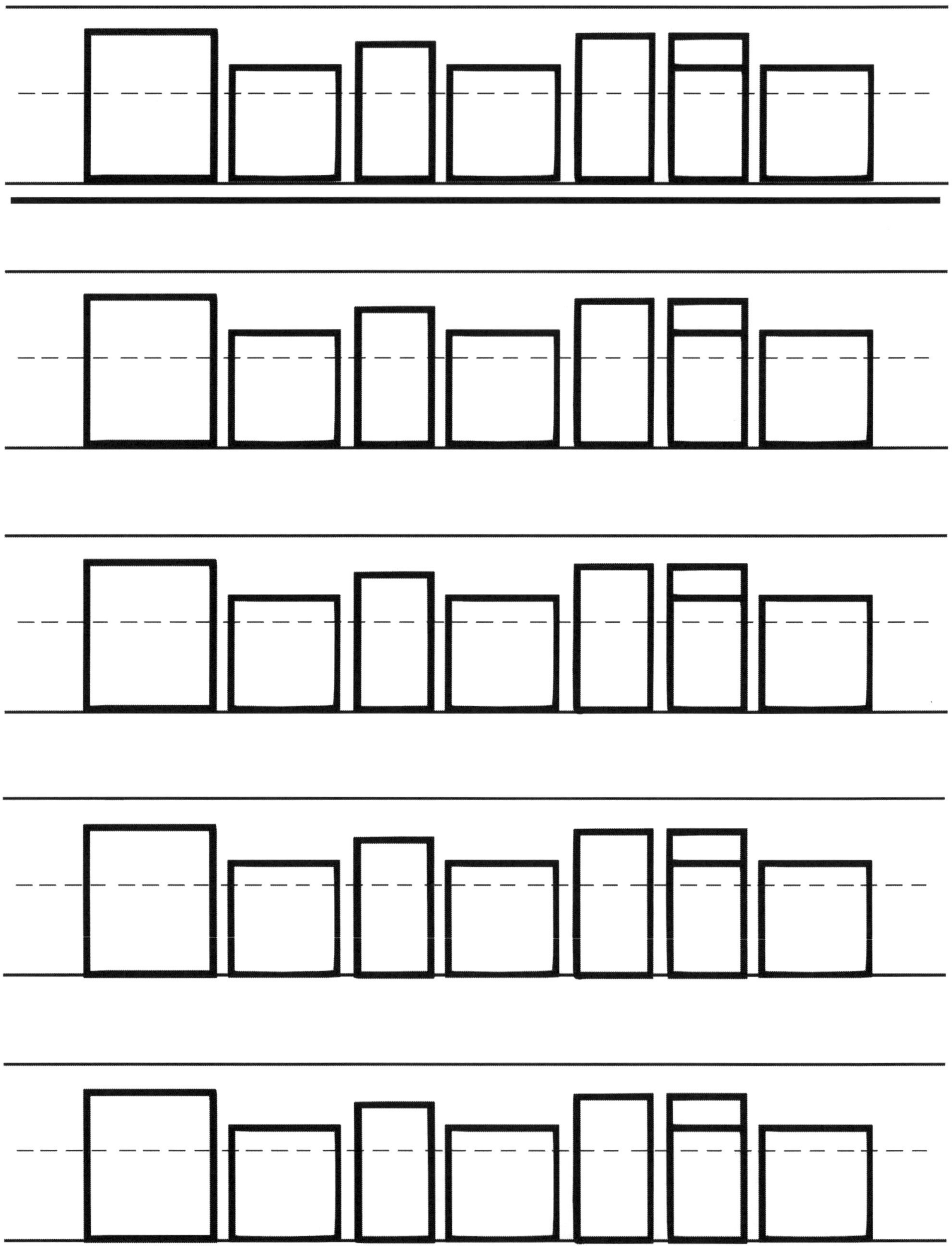

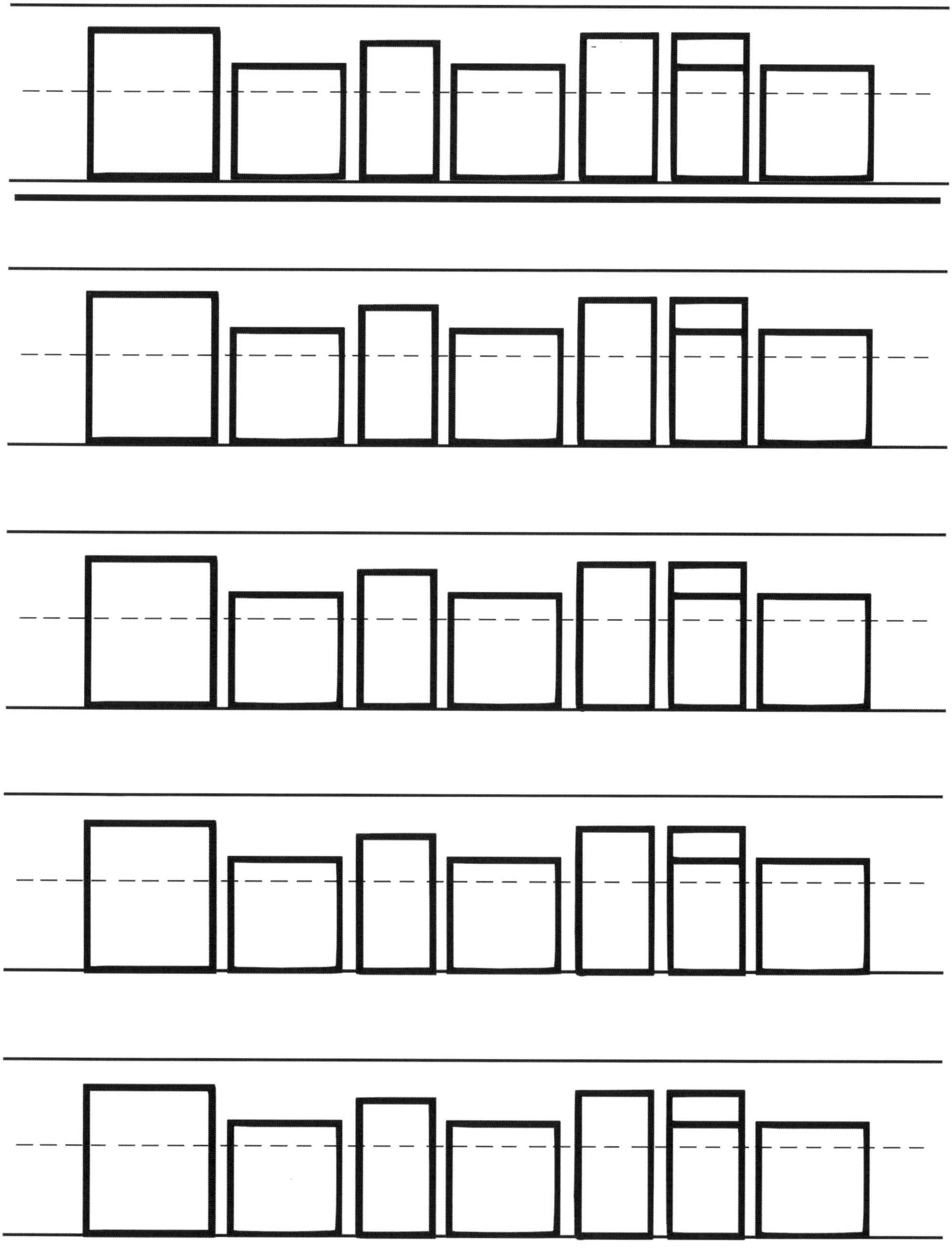

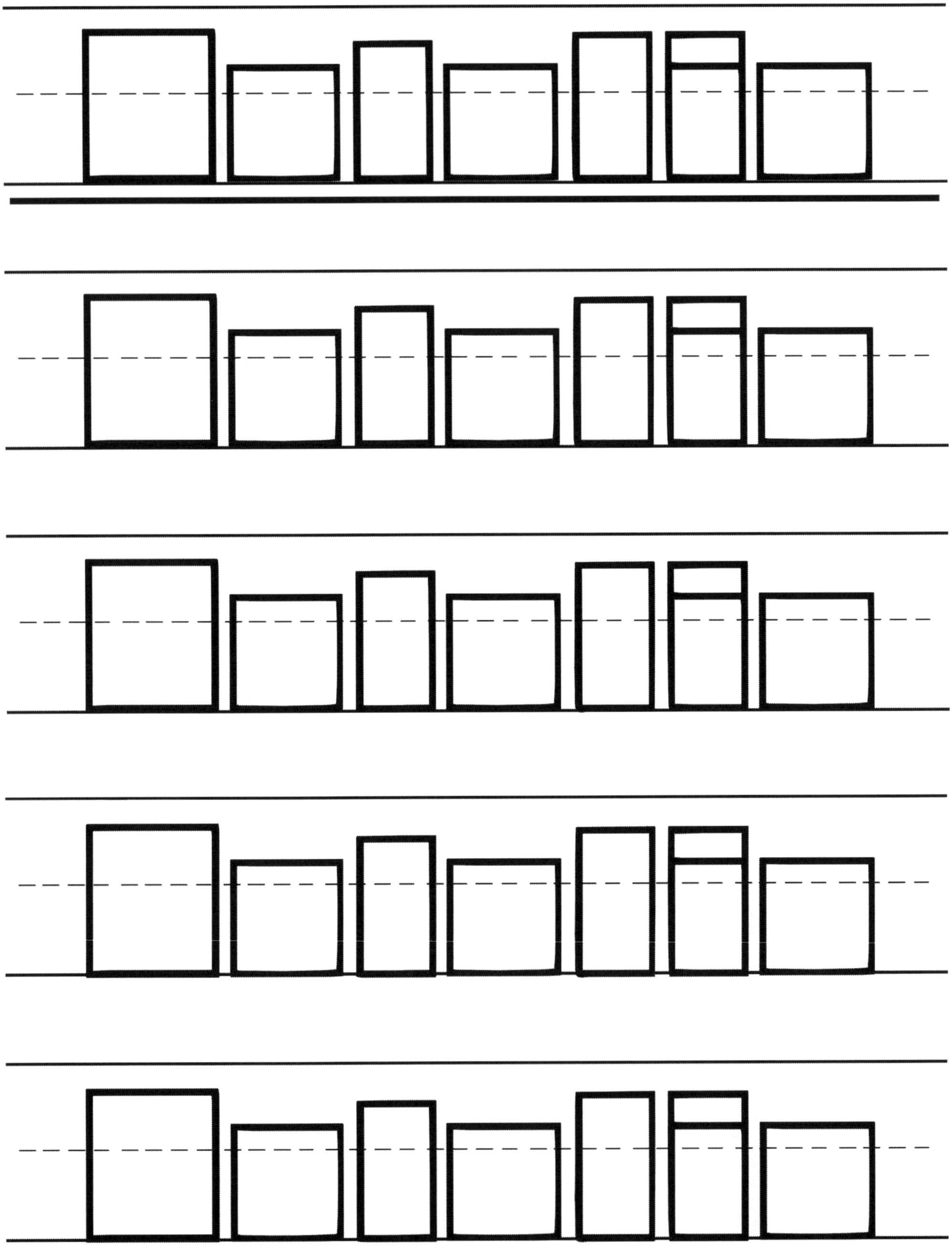

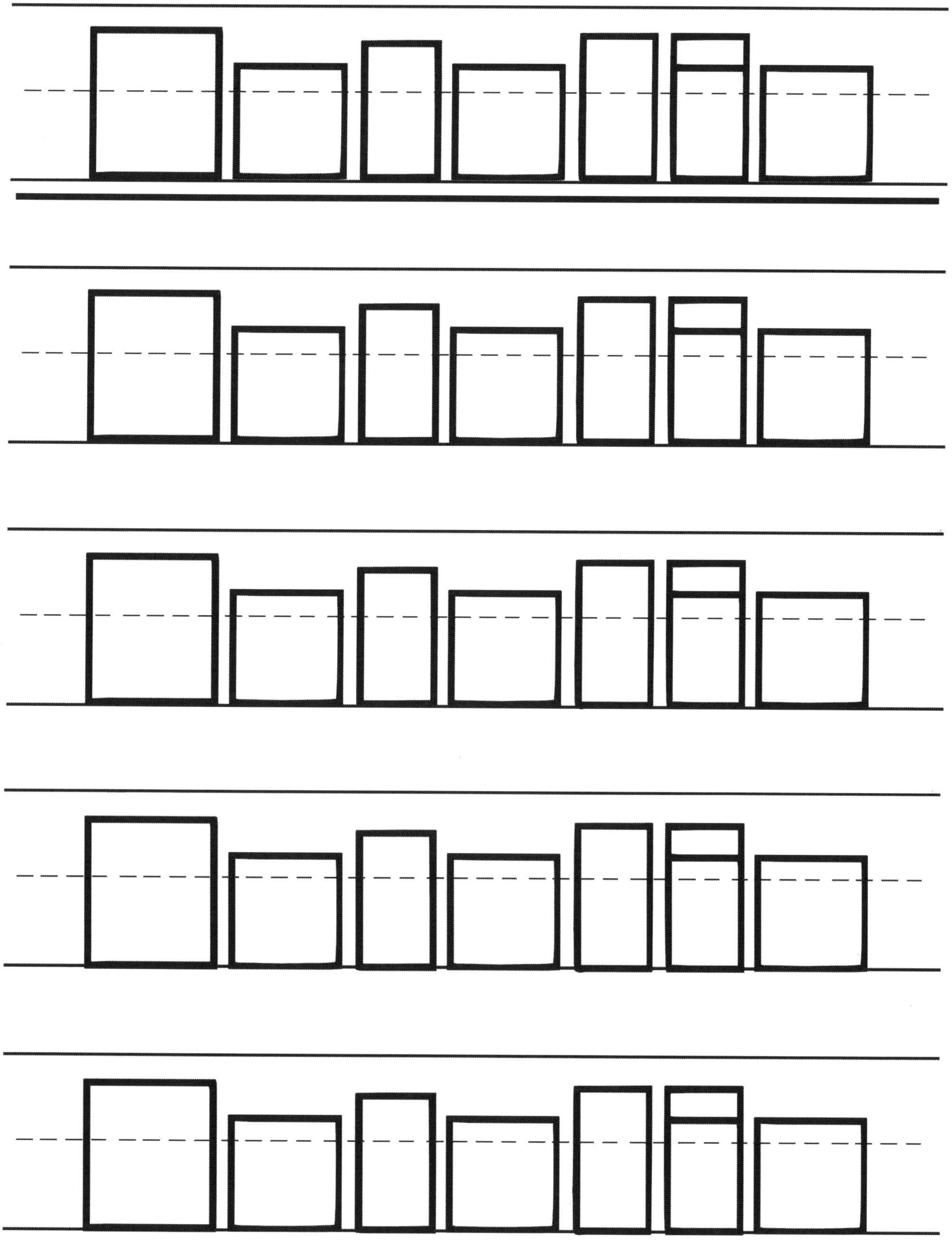

Natalie

Natalie

Natalie

Natalie

Natalie

Natalie

Natalie

Natalie

Natalie

Natalie

Natalie

Natalie

Natalie

Natalie

Natalie

Natalie

Natalie

Natalie

Natalie

Natalie

Natalie

Natalie

Natalie

Natalie

Natalie

Natalie

Natalie

Natalie

Natalie

Natalie

Natalie

Natalie

Natalie

Natalie

Natalie

Natalie

Natalie

Natalie

Natalie

Natalie

Natalie

Natalie

Natalie

Natalie

Natalie

Made in the USA
Columbia, SC
26 November 2023

27067084R00057